SCIENCE SKILLS 5

 **LIVING THINGS**

1 **Are the sentences *true* or *false*?**

  a Size is not important to life. Microscopic organisms are living things.   <u> true </u>

  b Everything that can move is living.   <u>   </u>

  c There are six characteristics of living things.   <u>   </u>

  d Not all living things can reproduce.   <u>   </u>

  e During their lives, living things grow larger.   <u>   </u>

  f Some living things make energy from the sun, but others need
    to take in energy from other organisms.   <u>   </u>

2 **There has been a mix-up in the lab! Unscramble the letters and label the cell structures. Which diagram is the animal cell and which is the plant cell?**

cuuelsn   tspoolhaclr   ualecvo   sypcoamlt   ecll bnmearem   lecl alwl

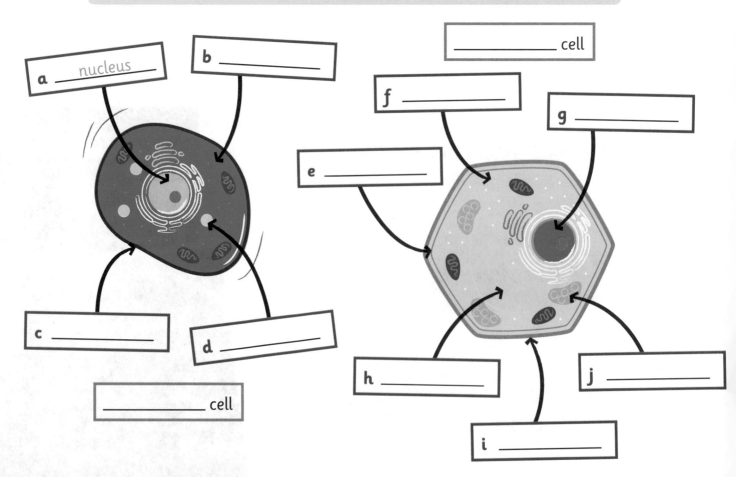

3 Write the name of the cell structure next to the description of its job in the cell.

a It stores substances in a cell. _____vacuole_____

b It contains all the cell structures and helps to give the cell shape. _____

c It controls the substances that go in and out of the cell. _____

d It controls the cell and contains all the genetic information. _____

e It supports the cell and provides strength. _____

f It helps the plant change light energy into food. _____

4 Read the text and choose the correct answer for each gap.

How do plants move?

All **(a)** ..... things can move. Although plants are not as obvious as animals, they move quite a bit. The flowers on a plant **(b)** ..... to light and can open during the day and close at **(c)** ..... . Leaves can also move and turn towards the sun, **(d)** ..... means that they get extra light to make food. Some flowers, like sunflowers, even seem to follow the sun.

Most plant movements are invisible to the naked eye; we need a **(e)** ..... to see them. The underside of a plant leaf is covered with tiny holes, called stomata. These open and close to **(f)** ..... substances in and out. Smaller still are the movements inside the plant. Plants, like humans, have a transport system that moves important substances around. The next time you see a plant, watch closely. It **(g)** ..... be moving before your very eyes!

a non-living / living / organism

b want / respond / bring

c morning / evening / night

d which / when / who

e thermometer / microscope / calculator

f allow / block / decide

g must / shouldn't / might

5 Complete the table.

	Composition	Function	Example
Cell	Single cell		Muscle cell
Tissue	Layers of cells		
Organ		They have a specific job to do in the body	
System	Different organs working together		Circulatory system

6 Write and draw to make a fact card about a living thing. Work with a partner and take turns to guess.

Who am I?

Appearance:

_____

_____

_____

Number of cells:

_____

_____

_____

Source of energy:

_____

_____

_____

7 Find the words. Then, write definitions for the words (a–e) listed below.

cell cytoplasm living thing multicellular nucleus
organ organism system tissue unicellular

m	u	l	t	i	c	e	l	l	u	l	a	r	q	b
c	u	h	l	i	v	i	n	g	t	h	i	n	g	z
e	y	n	p	h	v	b	o	i	d	u	d	v	c	q
y	o	t	i	b	o	b	r	b	n	o	j	f	m	l
v	r	u	o	c	a	e	q	f	r	s	g	h	k	x
b	g	t	m	p	e	y	z	b	g	w	d	l	w	s
v	a	t	h	u	l	l	n	n	c	z	b	t	u	y
x	n	r	i	d	x	a	l	h	e	j	r	e	y	s
c	i	o	t	s	x	f	s	u	l	z	l	q	w	t
u	s	t	o	i	s	g	t	m	l	c	e	y	k	e
o	m	j	j	u	t	u	v	o	u	a	l	b	s	m
o	r	g	a	n	f	c	e	n	a	x	r	a	f	j

a living thing: _____

_____

b cell: _____

_____

c multicellular: _____

_____

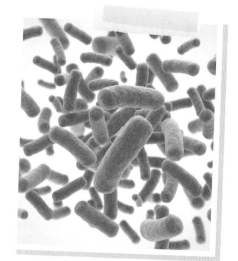

d organism: _____

_____

e cytoplasm: _____

_____

8 Amanda is looking through the newspaper at the adverts.
Choose the best organism for each advert.

1

Roommate wanted
Must make own food, have a cell wall and be multicellular.

a Mushroom
b Flower
c Bacteria

2

Small space available
Must be microscopic and unicellular.

a Giant kelp
b Bacteria
c Jellyfish

3

Help wanted
Organism recycling. No plants allowed.
Should be multicellular.

a Mushroom
b Flower
c Bacteria

4

Lost pet
Name: Squishy.
No cell wall. No spinal column. Great swimmer!

a Jellyfish
b Lion
c Flower

9 Circle the odd one out. Write an explanation.

a cell / tissue / organ / kingdom

A kingdom is different because it's a
form of classification. The others are
all parts of an organism.

b platypus / ostrich / lion / snake

_____

_____

c spider / Venus flytrap / lizard / cow

_____

_____

_____

d nucleus / cell wall / vacuole / cytoplasm

_____

_____

10 **Read the text about the weird and wonderful organism, the lichen. Write the correct word in each gap, then answer the questions.**

Most people confuse lichens with moss (the bushy green stuff on trees), **(a)** __but__ beware, these two organisms are very different!

Lichens are a complex living thing. **(b)** _____ are made up of two different organisms: a fungus and an alga. These organisms live together in a symbiotic relationship, each benefitting **(c)** _____ the other. The fungus is the central part, giving the lichen **(d)** _____ of its characteristics and providing the organism's structure. The algae can photosynthesise, so they provide the food. There are two different types of algae that live in a lichen. **(e)** _____ one is coloured: green algae and blue-green algae.

Besides their beauty, lichens **(f)** _____ important for our planet. Likes plants, **(g)** _____ convert carbon dioxide to oxygen. So, without the help of lichens, Earth would be **(h)** _____ little less airy!

i Are lichens the same as moss? Why / Why not?

_____

j What is a symbiotic relationship?

_____

k Can lichens make their own food? How?

_____

l Which of the five kingdoms does lichen belong to? Explain your answer.

_____

11 **Write whether the sentences describe *living things*, *non-living things* or *both*.**

a Things that do not need nutrients.   __non-living things__

b Things that breathe.   _____

c Things that produce waste.   _____

d Things that do not breathe air.   _____

e Things that are made up of cells, tissues, organs and systems. _____

f Things that can move.   _____

g Things that are classified into kingdoms.   _____

2 ECOSYSTEMS

1 Identify the ecosystems and write an example of each.

a

_____
_____

b

_____
_____

c

_____
_____

d

_____
_____

e

_____
_____

f

_____
_____

2 Write the living and non-living components of a savannah ecosystem in the correct category. Can you add any more?

rocks   trees   grass   zebra

Biotic factors	Abiotic factors
_____	_____
_____	_____
_____	_____
_____	_____
_____	_____

3 Draw an example for each word.

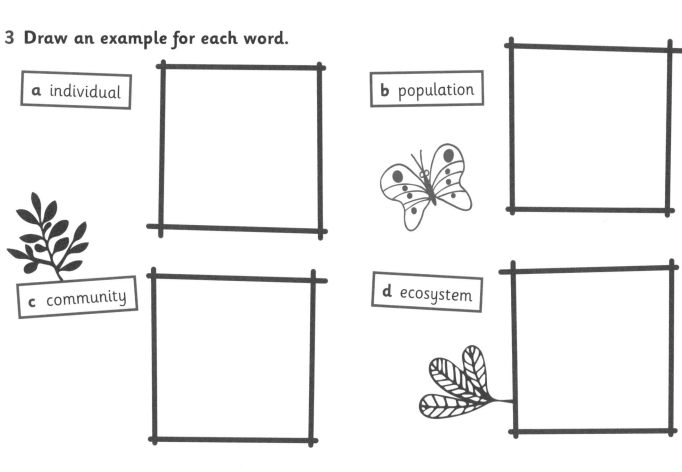

a individual

b population

c community

d ecosystem

4 How important are abiotic factors in an ecosystem? Consider the effect of the following actions:

a A family visits a river. It is hot and the children want to swim.
They build a small wall in the river with rocks to make a pool.

_____

_____

_____

b There is a terrible storm, causing a boat to sink to the bottom of the lake.
It is full of oil that is slowly leaking.

_____

_____

_____

c After a big rainstorm, there is a landslide on the side of a mountain.
Everything is covered in mud.

_____

_____

_____

5 **Complete the sentences.**

climate   fauna   flora   habitat   interact

   a Living things from the five kingdoms _____ with each other in an ecosystem.

   b The _____ is the general weather conditions of a region.

   c The living things in an ecosystem can be divided into _____ and _____ .

   d The area or environment in which an organism normally lives is known
     as the _____ .

6 **Think of the similarities and differences between these two grassland ecosystems. Write them in the correct place.**

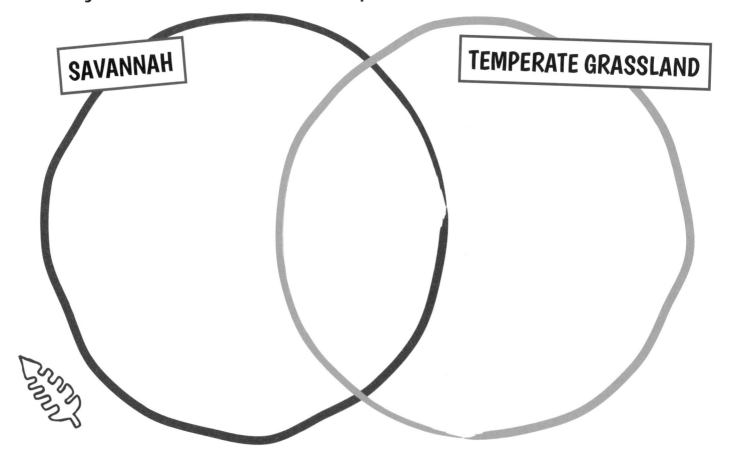

SAVANNAH

TEMPERATE GRASSLAND

7 **Write whether the sentences describe *grasslands* or *forests*.**

   a These require a rainy climate. _____

   b These contain few trees. _____

   c These are home to some of the largest fauna on land. _____

   d These are where over half of the species on Earth can be found. _____

8 Identify the ecosystems. Write a paragraph comparing and contrasting them.

a _____
_____
_____
_____

b _____
_____
_____
_____

9 Where can you find living things with these adaptations? Write them in the correct ecosystem. Can you add any other adaptations?

thick fur   nocturnal   spines   thick layer of fat   brown fur   white fur

Desert	Tundra

10 Complete the crossword using words from the unit.

DOWN

1 A large animal with lots of teeth that lives in a freshwater ecosystem.

2 A large protist that lives in a marine ecosystem.

3 A body of freshwater that flows from one place to another.

6 Home to about a quarter of marine life.

8 Small body of water with a variety of aquatic life.

ACROSS

4 The largest ecosystem on Earth.

5 Amphibian that lives in a freshwater ecosystem.

7 Where land and water meet.

9 Invertebrate that can stick to the surface of rocks.

10 Coral reefs provide this for many marine animals.

11 Read the text about city animals and choose the correct answer.

Left home for the city

As cities grow larger and natural places get smaller, more animals are moving into urban areas. Mice, rats and ants are very successful urban animals, but bigger animals, such as bears and coyotes are starting to move too.

In some places, bears look for food in rubbish bins rather than scavenging in forests. Coyotes have been spotted in every corner of the United States, including New York City. The ability of these animals to adapt is amazing. They have even learnt where to safely cross roads, so that they do not get run over by cars.

Scientists have found that city birds demonstrate *street smarts*. This means they have more knowledge to deal with an urban environment. Some can even open containers better than their wild cousins. Who knows what urban ecosystems will look like in the future and which animals will become our neighbours!

1 Animals are moving into urban areas because:
   a cities are getting smaller.
   b natural habitats are reducing in size.
   c they prefer to be around people.

2 Bears look for food:
   a in rubbish bins.
   b in New York City.
   c in taxis.

3 How have coyotes learnt to survive in cities?
   a They have learnt to open containers.
   b They have learnt to drive cars.
   c They have learnt to safely cross roads.

4 Where have coyotes been seen?
   a Only in New York City.
   b On street corners.
   c All over the USA.

5 City birds with street smarts:
   a live longer than birds in natural habitats.
   b know how to deal with living in the city.
   c have difficulty finding containers.

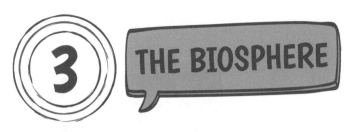

3 THE BIOSPHERE

1 Are the following sentences examples of *competition* or *cooperation*?

a Bees live in a hive and have an organised society where each insect has a special role. _____

b On the jungle floor, some plants grow faster than others to reach the sunlight. _____

c Male peacocks grow beautiful feathers to impress female peacocks. _____

d Cleaner shrimps pick particles from the surface of other animals to eat. _____

e In the Antarctic, Emperor penguins huddle together and move in a circle to keep warm. _____

f Lions and hyenas in the Serengeti fight for better hunting areas. _____

g Fish live in a group, called a school, for protection. _____

2 Now write another example of each.

Competition:

_____

_____

_____

Cooperation:

_____

_____

_____

3 Complete the table.

secondary   2nd   first   third   tertiary   1st

			primary
	second		
3rd			

4 Label the photos according to the roles in the food chain. Add arrows to complete the food chain.

_____

_____

_____

_____

_____

_____

5 Read the example then describe two relationships from the food chain above.

In a forest food chain, the grass is eaten by the rabbit, which is then eaten by the fox.
The rabbit is a primary consumer and the fox is a secondary consumer.

a

_____

_____

_____

b

_____

_____

_____

6 Complete the crossword using words from the unit.

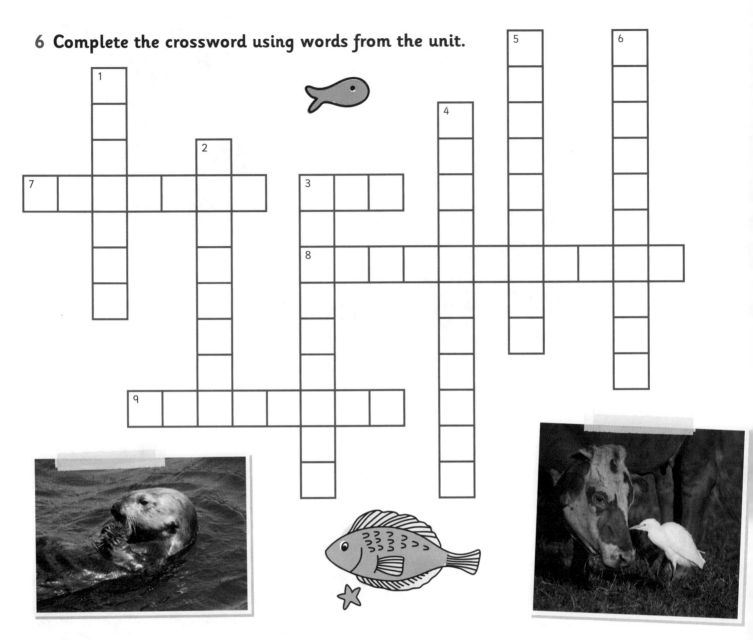

DOWN

1 A specific place where an organism lives.

2 A living thing that gets its energy from the sun.

3 A _____ consumer eats herbivores.

4 When two living things fight for resources.

5 A _____ shows us how energy passes from the sun to a consumer.

6 A living thing that breaks down dead things into organic matter.

ACROSS

3 The _____ provides energy to producers.

7 A _____ consumer eats producers.

8 When living things help each other.

9 A _____ consumer is at the end of a food chain.

7 Look at the food web in the Pupil's Book and write the living things in the correct column. Some may go in more than one column.

BAMBOO   BAT   CAPYBARA   TOUCAN   LEAFCUTTER ANT

HOWLER MONKEY   ANTEATER   RED-EYED TREE FROG

TERMITE   CAIMAN   GREEN ANACONDA   JAGUAR

FUNGI   BANANA TREE   BACTERIA

Producers	Primary consumers	Secondary consumers	Tertiary consumers	Decomposers

8 Create a food web using the living things in the box. Draw and label each living thing. Add arrows between them.

grass snake mouse lizard
hawk grasshopper rabbit

Look at your food web. Give one example of:

a a predator _____

b prey _____

c competition _____

_____

grass

9 Order the words to make sentences.

a global / the / biosphere / is / ecosystem. / The

_____

b host. / on / parasite / A / a / relies

_____

c and / dead / plants / Scavengers / animals. / eat

_____

d each / things / in / global / with / Living / other / ecosystem. / interact / the

_____

10 Read about the Gulf oil spill. Choose the correct answer for each gap.

A sticky mess!

The Gulf oil spill started **(a)** ..... April 20, 2010 **(b)** ..... the Gulf of Mexico about 67 kilometres **(c)** ..... the coast of Louisiana. The leak lasted **(d)** ..... 87 days. About 3.19 million barrels **(e)** ..... oil leaked **(f)** ..... the ocean. Many species were affected **(g)** ..... the spill. Dolphins, seabirds and fish were covered **(h)** ..... oil, but it will be many more years **(i)** ..... we see all the effects of the oil spill on the environment.

a on / in / at

b on / in / at

c at / from / on

d for / of / from

e for / of / from

f to / in / into

g by / of / with

h by / of / with

i before / by / from

11 Are the sentences *true* or *false*?

a Global warming is when the Earth's temperature decreases because of human activity. _____

b Farming is the main reason for deforestation. _____

c Species can grow in their natural habitat when cities get larger. _____

d Cars and large factories pollute the environment, which can kill living things. _____

e When species become extinct, there is more biodiversity. _____

12 Read the descriptions of the national parks. Choose the correct answer for each question.

Etosha National Park, in Namibia, covers an area of 22,270 square kilometres. It has a savannah climate with high temperatures and very little rain. It is home to many species, but the plants are mainly shrubs and grasses.

Shey Phoksundo National Park is set high up in the Himalayas. The area is rocky and is an important home to many endangered animals. The winters are difficult, preventing large human populations from settling.

Bwindi National Park has one of the most diverse forests in East Africa, including 163 species of trees. It has a tropical climate and a very rugged landscape with narrow valleys, rivers and steep hills.

Which national park:

a is located at high altitude?   Etosha / Shey Phoksundo / Bwindi

b is a grassland ecosystem?   Etosha / Shey Phoksundo / Bwindi

c has high temperatures and lots of rain?   Etosha / Shey Phoksundo / Bwindi

d is not found in Africa?   Etosha / Shey Phoksundo / Bwindi

e is flatter than the others?   Etosha / Shey Phoksundo / Bwindi

4 **ENERGY**

1 Look at the pictures. Write the form of energy.

a

b

c

_____ _____ _____

d

e

f

_____ _____ _____

2 Label the diagram with the correct forms of energy and answer the questions.

a _____

b _____

c _____

d How is kinetic energy different from potential energy?

_____

_____

e Give an example of potential energy.

_____

_____

f What is mechanical energy?

_____

_____

3 **Look at the three photos. Describe what is happening and the energy transformations that are involved. Write 35 words or more.**

_____

_____

_____

_____

_____

_____

4 Complete the sentences.

a Energy cannot be _____ or _____ .

b Energy changes from one form to another. This is called energy _____ .

c When energy transformations are not useful, we say the energy is _____ or _____ .

d An example of energy transformation is when a car _____ the chemical energy stored in fuel to _____ energy so it can move.

5 **Write definitions for the words below.**

   a Non-renewable energy:

   _____

   _____

   b Renewable energy:

   _____

   _____

6 **Match words from each of the three categories. Use a different colour for each.**

Renewable energy	Source	Type of energy
solar	wind	light
wind	heat from Earth's core	thermal
geothermal	the sun	mechanical
hydropower	organic material	mechanical
biomass	moving water	thermal

7 **Write whether the characteristics describe solar energy, wind energy or both.**

   a Converts mechanical energy into electricity. _____

   b Produces no air pollution. _____

   c A form of renewable energy. _____

   d Changes light into electricity. _____

   e Is found in nature. _____

   f Is produced with a turbine. _____

8 Read the text about geothermal energy in Iceland. Choose the correct answer for each gap.

Bubbling with energy

Iceland is a world leader in geothermal energy and gets almost all its energy from **(a)** ..... sources. Iceland is located on a crack in the Earth´s crust so **(b)** ..... energy from the Earth's core rises and **(c)** ..... enormous underground reservoirs of water to more than 300°C. Wells are drilled into the reservoirs and steam rises to power stations. The steam is then used to turn **(d)** ..... and make **(e)** ..... . The thermal energy is used to provide hot water to the cities. There is no air pollution or radiation, so it is a safe and clean process.

a renewable / radiation / fossil fuel

b electric / chemical / thermal

c heats / melts / moves

d solar panels / turbines / wheels

e light / heat / electricity

9 Fossil fuels or nuclear energy? Write *F* or *N*.

Source		Risks	
Coal	☐	Acid rain	☐
Uranium	☐	Water pollution	☐
Natural gas	☐	Radiation	☐
Oil	☐	Toxic waste	☐
		Global warming	☐

10 Complete the crossword using words from the unit.

DOWN

1 Energy created using the movement of a river.

4 The device that converts wind into electricity.

6 A form of energy that transforms heat from the Earth's core.

8 Energy that travels in waves through the air.

ACROSS

2 Precipitation that pollutes.

3 A form of energy that helps us to see.

5 A renewable energy whose source is organic material.

7 Oil, coal and natural gas.

9 The source of nuclear power.

10 The device used to transform sunlight into electricity.

11 Energy used by our bodies to live.

11 **Think about your class project to convince your family to save energy.**
Write an email to your friend James. Write 25 words or more.

In the email:
- tell James about your energy-saving project.
- say some of ways you can save energy.
- ask him if he knows any other ways to save energy.

_____

_____

_____

_____

_____

12 **Are you a waster or a saver? Answer the questions by circling a number for each one.**

a How often do you use public transport?
   Always = 4   Usually = 3   Sometimes = 2   Never = 1

b How often do you completely shut down tablets or computers?
   Always = 4   Usually = 3   Sometimes = 2   Never = 1

c How often do you turn the lights off when you leave a room?
   Always = 4   Usually = 3   Sometimes = 2   Never = 1

d How often do you recycle?
   Always = 4   Usually = 3   Sometimes = 2   Never = 1

e How often do you choose eco-friendly products?
   Always = 4   Usually = 3   Sometimes = 2   Never = 1

Add up your points to see your energy-saving status.

15–20 points: Super-saver!

10–15 points: Keep up the good work. You just need to make a few more changes.

5–10 points: Time for you to start saving more. The Earth needs you!

5 points: You are using too much energy! Just a few changes and you can
                be super too!

5 SOUND, LIGHT AND HEAT

1 Look at the photos. Which forms of energy are shown: *heat*, *light* or *sound*? You can write more than one.

a

_____

b

_____

c

_____

d

_____

e

_____

f

_____

2 Are the sentences *true* or *false*?

a Sound travels in waves.   _____

b Sound does not travel in space because there is no gravity there.   _____

c Sound can travel in all directions.   _____

d Sound can travel through different materials.   _____

e Sound travels slower through water than through air.   _____

f Large vibrations are perceived as soft sounds.   _____

3 Some sounds are pleasant and we enjoy hearing them. Other sounds are annoying and we cannot stand them! Write examples from each category from your own experiences.

I enjoy the sound of …

_____
_____
_____
_____
_____

I cannot stand the sound of …

_____
_____
_____
_____
_____

4 Order the words to make sentences about light.

a found / sources / nature. / in / light / are / Natural

_____

b man-made. / Artificial / sources / light / are

_____

c sun. / main / Our / the / light / source / of / is / natural

_____

d light / A / artificial / is / lightbulb / an / source.

_____

5 Match the sentence halves about the properties of light.

a Light energy travels in …   … 300,000 kilometres per second.

b Light from the sun takes …   … straight lines called rays.

c Light energy travels at …   … with an object, it is absorbed, reflected or refracted.

d When light comes into contact …   … 8 minutes and 20 seconds to reach the Earth.

e A ray of light contains …   … all colours.

6 Read the text and choose the correct answer for each gap.

Properties of light

As humans, the colours we perceive are called **(a)** ..... light. When light comes into contact with an object, the light can be absorbed, **(b)** ..... or refracted. For example, when a **(c)** ..... of light comes into contact with a particular object, the object appears green. This is because the green light is **(d)** ..... , while all the other colours are **(e)** ..... . When light passes through a medium with a different **(f)** ..... , it changes direction. This is called **(g)** ..... .

a invisible / infrared / visible

b transformed / reflected / seen

c shine / ray / arrow

d reflected / transformed / absorbed

e seen / absorbed / reflected

f density / size / colour

g refract / refraction / refracted

7 Explain what is happening in each of the pictures.

28

8 Write your own definition of refraction. Give examples of how refraction is used in daily life.

_____

_____

_____

_____

_____

9 Write whether the sentences describe *refraction* or *reflection*.

a You see yourself in a calm lake.   _____

b A coin looks bigger when placed in water.   _____

c A straw looks bent in water.   _____

d You see yourself in the bathroom mirror.   _____

10 It is a cold day in winter and you leave your bedroom window open. Your grandmother says to you "*Close the window! You're letting the cold in!*" What is incorrect about her statement?

_____

_____

_____

11 Circle the correct answer for each question.

1 You have two glasses with ice cubes in them. Both are in the shade, but you cover one with a sock. In which glass will the ice melt slower?

   a The ice in the covered glass will melt slower because the sock is a thermal insulator.

   b The ice in both glasses will melt at the same rate because the sock has no effect.

   c The ice in the uncovered glass will melt slower because there is no sock to heat it.

2 You have two bowls of water. One bowl is made of stone and the other is made of metal. If you set them both on a stove, which bowl will the water evaporate from first?

   a From the stone bowl because it is a better thermal insulator.

   b From the metal bowl because it is a better thermal conductor.

   c From the stone bowl because it is a better thermal conductor.

12 Write three ways that heat affects matter. Give an example and draw an illustration for each.

Way heat affects matter	Example	Illustration

13 Write the letters (a – i) in the Venn diagram.

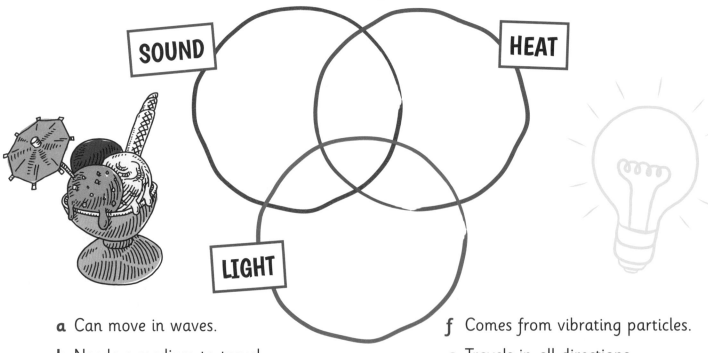

SOUND

HEAT

LIGHT

a Can move in waves.

b Needs a medium to travel.

c Comes from the sun.

d Has natural and artificial sources.

e Travels at 300,000 kilometres per second.

f Comes from vibrating particles.

g Travels in all directions.

h Travels in a straight line.

i Can change the state of matter of an object.

14 Solve the word problems using your knowledge of sound, light and heat.

Party time

You are going to a party! You are in charge of bringing hot soup and ice cream. It takes 30 minutes to walk there and it is a hot day. Think of a plan to keep the soup hot and the ice cream from melting. You must walk to the party and can only use things you would find around the house.

_____

_____

_____

A terrible night and a big exam

You have got a big exam tomorrow. You need to get some sleep, but your neighbours are having a loud party. Your bedroom window is broken and it is very cold outside. The light in your bedroom will not turn off! Without leaving your bedroom, what can you do to reduce the noise and light and stay warm all night?

_____

_____

_____

The key

Silly you! You left your keys in the freezer and they are now frozen in a block of ice. You need to open the door so that you can go to school. What can you do to melt the ice as quickly as possible without using artificial heat sources like an oven or microwave?

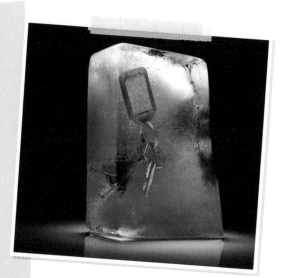

_____

_____

_____

6 ELECTRICITY

1 Label the atom using the words and symbols.

neutron   proton   electron   +   0   –

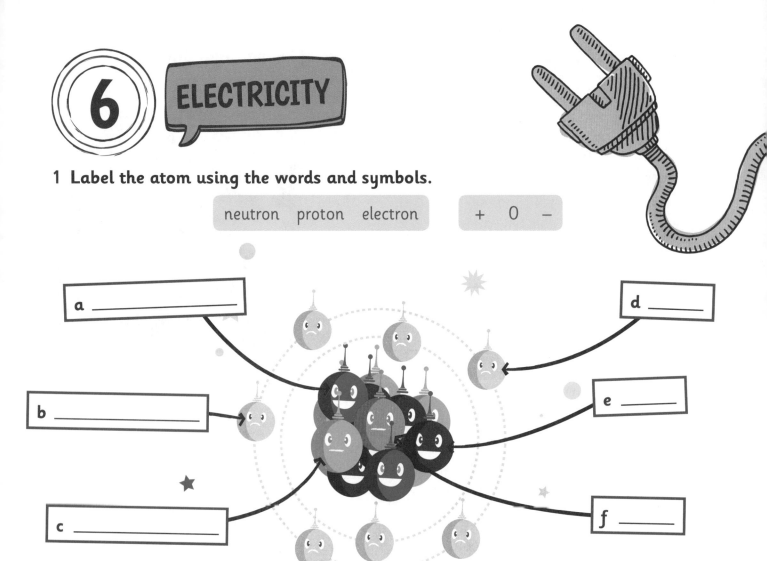

a _____

b _____

c _____

d _____

e _____

f _____

2 Look at the pictures. Write whether the objects are *positively charged*, *negatively charged* or *electrically neutral*.

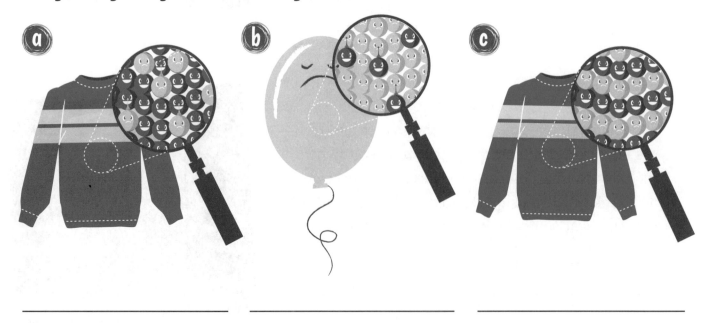

a _____   b _____   c _____

3 **Write sentences about the objects from Activity 2.**

  a What happens when the balloon is placed near the first jumper (Jumper a)?

  _____

  b What happens when the balloon is placed next to another identically charged balloon?

  _____

  c Have all the items got a charge?

  _____

4 **Read the text below and write the correct word in each gap.**

Fast-moving ice and water particles bump into **(a)** _____ other in a storm cloud. This creates static electrical charges. When the charge is strong enough, the energy is released. It goes to the ground or to another **(b)** _____ , looking for an opposite **(c)** _____ . This is seen as a lightning bolt. The lighting heats the air around it very quickly, causing a loud boom, called **(d)** _____ . Three forms of energy are released during a storm: light, sound and **(e)** _____ . Lightning and thunder occur at the same time, but because light travels faster than sound, we see the lightning before we **(f)** _____ the thunder.

5 **Are the sentences _true_ or _false_?**

  a Static electricity is the flow of electrons through a material. _____

  b Static electricity is caused by an imbalance of charges between two electrical insulators. _____

  c Most electric machines run on static electricity. _____

  d Rubbing non-metal objects together creates electric current. _____

  e A positively charged object is attracted to a negatively charged object. _____

  f You can feel a small shock when lots of electrons move at the same time. _____

6 Write the materials in the correct column. Add some of your own ideas.

rubber   plastic   copper   wood   aluminium

Insulators	Conductors
_____	_____
_____	_____
_____	_____
_____	_____
_____	_____
_____	_____
_____	_____
_____	_____

7 Label the diagram using these words.

power source   wire   switch   resistor

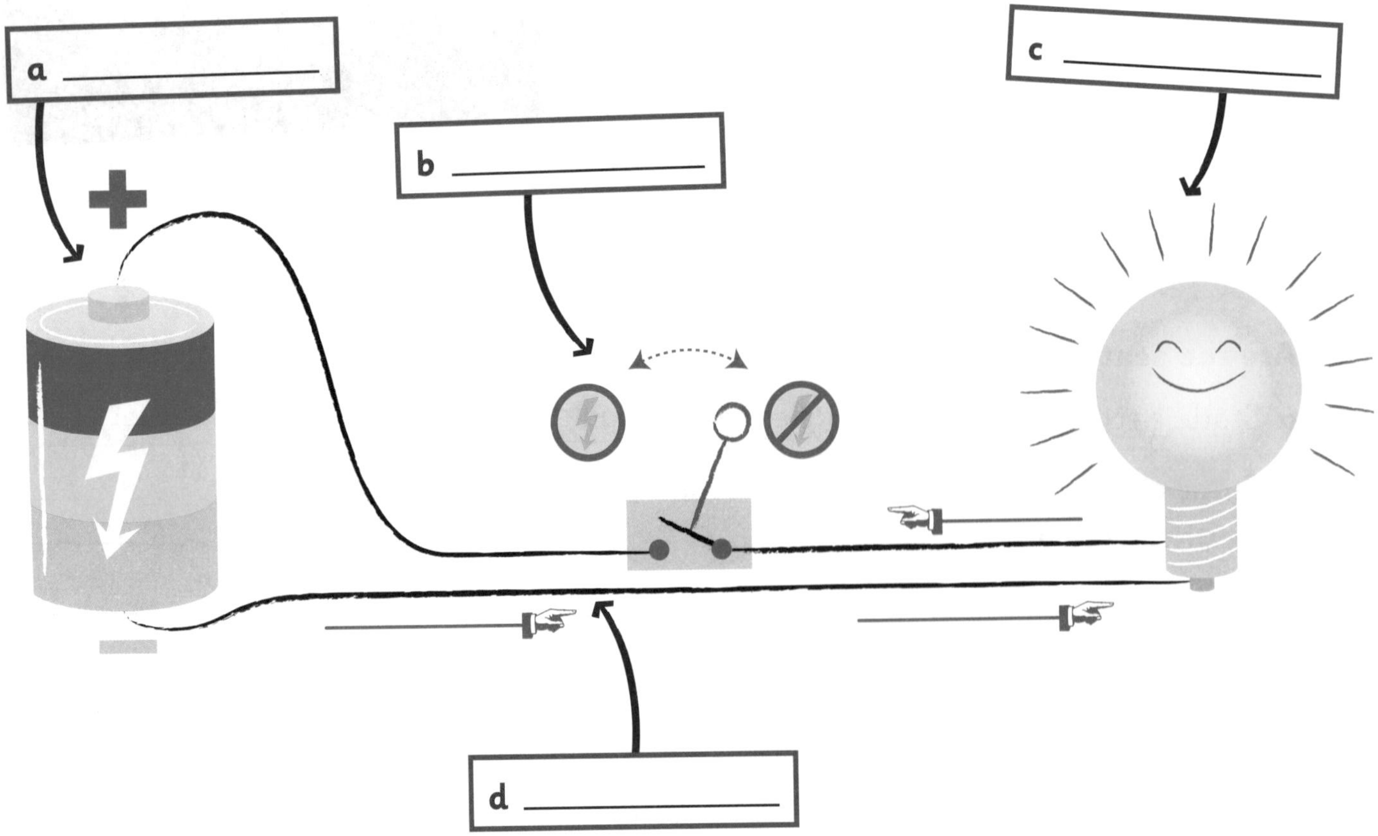

a _____

b _____

c _____

d _____

8 Write the vocabulary from Activity 7 next to the correct description.

a It conducts electricity. _____

b It provides the electricity. _____

c It transforms electricity into other forms of energy. _____

d It opens or closes the circuit. _____

9 You start building an electrical circuit, but you realise that you have not got enough wire! Write three things you could use to complete the circuit. Explain your choices and decide which one would work best.

_____

_____

_____

_____

_____

_____

10 Choose one of these inventions and answer the questions.

lightbulb   telephone   movie camera

a How does this invention help people?

_____

_____

b How do you think it has changed the way people live?

_____

_____

c What did the inventor need to know about to invent it?

_____

_____

11 Write the name of each invention under the photo. Match each photo to the inventor and function. Use a different colour for each one.

Inventors	Inventions	Function
Nikola Tesla	_____	It transforms chemical energy into electrical energy.
Alessandro Volta	_____	It transmits sound over air instead of through wires.
Alan Turing	_____	It allows electricity to travel longer distances through power lines.
Guglielmo Marconi	_____	It processes information and shows it on a screen.
Michael Faraday	_____	It transforms mechanical energy into electrical energy.

12 **Choose your favourite three inventions from the unit. Draw them and write why you chose each one.**

_____ _____ _____

_____ _____ _____

_____ _____ _____

13 **Read this email from your English-speaking friend, Bob, and the notes you have made. Write your email to Bob, using all the notes.**

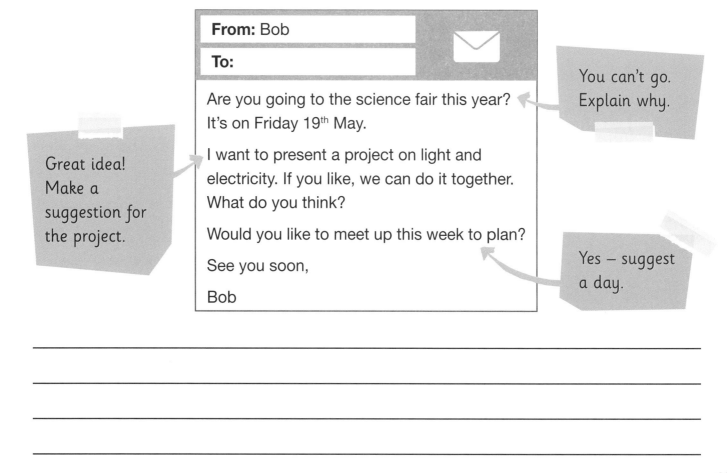

From: Bob

To:

Are you going to the science fair this year? It's on Friday 19th May.

You can't go. Explain why.

I want to present a project on light and electricity. If you like, we can do it together. What do you think?

Great idea! Make a suggestion for the project.

Would you like to meet up this week to plan?

See you soon,

Bob

Yes – suggest a day.

_____

_____

_____

_____

HOW DO YOU SAY ... ?

Unit 1: Living things

English	Your language
bacteria (n)	_____
cell (n)	_____
cell membrane (n)	_____
cell wall (n)	_____
chloroplast (n)	_____
classify (v)	_____
cytoplasm (n)	_____
fungus (n)	_____
Monera (n)	_____
multicellular (adj)	_____
nucleus (n)	_____
organ (n)	_____
organism (n)	_____
plant (n)	_____
protist (n)	_____
species (n)	_____
system (n)	_____
tissue (n)	_____
unicellular (adj)	_____
vacuole (n)	_____

Unit 2: Ecosystems

English	Your language
abiotic (adj)	_____
adapt (v)	_____
aquatic (adj)	_____
biotic (adj)	_____
climate (n)	_____
community (n)	_____
coral reef (n)	_____
desert (n)	_____
fauna (n)	_____
flora (n)	_____
forest (n)	_____
grassland (n)	_____
habitat (n)	_____
individual (n)	_____
nocturnal (adj)	_____
pond (n)	_____
population (n)	_____
shoreline (n)	_____
tundra (n)	_____
urban (adj)	_____

Unit 3: The biosphere

English	Your language
biodiversity (n)	_____
biosphere (n)	_____
competition (n)	_____
consumer (n)	_____
cooperation (n)	_____
decomposer (n)	_____
deforestation (n)	_____
endangered (adj)	_____
extinct (adj)	_____
food chain (n)	_____
food web (n)	_____
global warming (n)	_____
national park (n)	_____
nature reserve (n)	_____
oil spill (n)	_____
parasite (n)	_____
predator (n)	_____
prey (n)	_____
producer (n)	_____
scavenger (n)	_____

Unit 4: Energy

English	Your language
acid rain (n)	_____
biomass (n)	_____
chemical energy (n)	_____
electrical energy (n)	_____
fossil fuel (n)	_____
geothermal energy (n)	_____
hydropower (n)	_____
kinetic energy (n)	_____
light energy (n)	_____
mechanical energy (n)	_____
non-renewable (adj)	_____
nuclear power (n)	_____
potential energy (n)	_____
radioactive waste (n)	_____
renewable (adj)	_____
solar energy (n)	_____
sound energy (n)	_____
thermal energy (n)	_____
turbine (n)	_____
uranium (n)	_____

Unit 5: Sound, light and heat

English	Your language
absorb (v)	_____
bioluminescence (n)	_____
density (n)	_____
evaporate (v)	_____
expand (v)	_____
lens (n)	_____
melt (v)	_____
mirror (n)	_____
molecule (n)	_____
opaque (adj)	_____
ray (n)	_____
reflect (v)	_____
refract (v)	_____
speed of light (n)	_____
thermal conductor (n)	_____
thermal insulator (n)	_____
translucent (adj)	_____
transparent (adj)	_____
vacuum (n)	_____
vibrate (v)	_____
wave (n)	_____

Unit 6: Electricity

English	Your language
atom (n)	_____
attract (v)	_____
battery (n)	_____
current electricity (n)	_____
discover (v)	_____
electron (n)	_____
flow (n)	_____
imbalance (n)	_____
invent (v)	_____
lightbulb (n)	_____
lightning (n)	_____
negatively charged (adj)	_____
neutron (n)	_____
nucleus (n)	_____
positively charged (adj)	_____
proton (n)	_____
repel (v)	_____
resistor (n)	_____
static electricity (n)	_____
switch (n)	_____
wire (n)	_____